Introduction

The library at Headington is not just a room that houses books. It is a vibrant place of learning, integrated into and supporting the curriculum across the whole school community. Open from 7.30am to 6.00pm, and staffed by two full-time librarians, it offers a relaxed and constructive learning environment where everyone is respected and valued.

It supports and encourages girls of all abilities and provides a research base for both staff and students alike. Through research, students learn how to search for, handle and interrogate information, in addition to referencing and bibliographic construction – essential skills that will hold them in good stead when entering Higher Education in the future.

Until summer 2016 the library was sited at the far west end of the first floor of the main school building, beyond the English Department. It was housed in a large purpose-built space and had become one of the school's focal points for learning. It was largely a traditional print school library and – despite continually developing online resources, initially designed to support out-of-hours academic needs – the library looked dated and was in need of modernisation (See Figs 1–3).

In early 2015 it was revealed that the strategic plan of senior management was to move the library from the first floor to the ground floor to a room originally built as the school gymnasium. This proposed move presented an opportunity to look in detail at its contents, and to move the focus from printed to digital resources. The move would enable the school to put in place a new state-of-the-art facility embracing new technology often found only in university libraries. This new library would support and enhance the wider aims of the school – part of which were to fully embrace and integrate new technology into teaching and learning.

Figs 1–3 – View of the old library. Photos by Lynn Winkworth.

Figs 4 and 5 – The old gymnasium, or Reading Room. Photos by Lynn Winkworth.

At the time of the proposed move the new location – the original school gymnasium – was an underused space; with its high-vaulted ceiling and arched windows it had a unique character that had remained unchanged for many years (Figs 4 and 5). It was used as an area for independent study, furnished with a few tables and computers, and was known as the Reading Room.

It was at this point I was approached and invited to become involved in the detailed planning. It was going to be an adventure!

Moving a school library and changing its focus is not to be undertaken lightly and required many hours of planning, research and preparation. All this had to happen while the existing library was still operating as usual – closing it before the physical move was not an option.

So, how did we go about it?

The vision

In developing our vision for the new library it was important to take full account of the direction the school was moving in and to look to its projected future. It was essential the new library encompassed and supported these plans to be a successful marriage of new technology with traditional printed sources; reflecting resources and equipment found in university libraries. Most of all, it needed to give our students the opportunity to develop new skills that would prepare them well for future study and the world of work.

To ensure the new library became a top-class study environment we agreed that it would be fully climate controlled, have adjustable LED lighting throughout, encompass cutting-edge technology, and would be fitted with bespoke furniture.

In order to realise this vision we would need to develop facilities not commonly found within the school environment.

So how did we achieve what we set out to do?

We began by thoroughly examining how the current library was used, in order to determine the essential requirements needed in the new space. Although this is not an exhaustive list, these are some of the areas we looked at:

- How many students use the library each day?
- In what way is the library used each day?
- What is the library's role in teaching and learning?
- What is the library's role in private study and the wider school community?
- What accommodation is required to meet study needs?
- How are printed resources currently used?
- How are electronic resources currently used?
- What is the role of technology within the library and how could it be developed further?
- How are study skills likely to develop in the future?

By examining every part of the library from its physical layout and facilities to its role in teaching and learning, a development plan gradually emerged.

Talking to other librarians and visiting other libraries was an important part of my research during the initial planning stages.

Birmingham Public Library, newly opened, enabled me to see how technology could positively enhance the library experience with their amazing interactive tables. The John Henry Brookes Library, newly opened at Oxford Brookes University, gave me an insight into how technology is used within university libraries – here I first saw smart issue and return systems at work. Kingham School library demonstrated how online fiction books (known as eBooks) can successfully enhance the printed collection, while Stowe School gave me an insight into how iPads were used within their school and the role the library played in supporting this initiative. My visit to Wellington College clearly demonstrated it was possible to successfully integrate electronic and printed resources to enhance learning.

We needed to encompass all I had discovered from my visits and more, if we were going to fully realise our vision of a new state-of-the-art library at Headington School.

Designing the space

After many meetings with the Bursar, my line manager and the architect – Anthony Pettorino – a design for the new library was created (see Fig. 6). To make the most of the unique space we would create a dramatic mezzanine that would sit within the vaulted ceiling, accessed by a sweeping staircase. A large glass extension would be added, extending the library seamlessly into the central quad and allowing in lots of natural light. Glass access points – discreet, short corridors – would connect the extension to the main library area, and a living roof of sedum would complete this part of the build. Columns of colour-changing LED lights in both the main area and extension would add additional interest while creating aesthetic consistency.

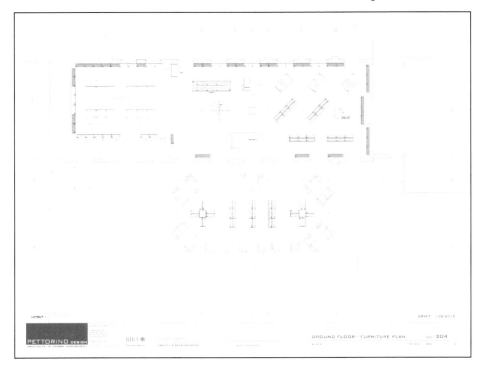

Fig. 6 – 'Library and Reading Room. Ground floor – furniture plan'. ©Pettorino Design

The existing building is part of the conservation area of the school, so any adaptations had to be looked at and undertaken very carefully to ensure all conservation regulations were met.

The design also encompassed the physical requirements needed to successfully manage the new library – a large working area for library staff and a walk-in store cupboard were successfully built into the design.

Planning the internal space proved challenging. We needed to incorporate not only bookshelves, but also study areas for the students. As part of our planning we visited St Helen and St Katherine School in Abingdon, which had recently invested in a purpose-built library. This visit proved very valuable, allowing us to see a newly finished school library that used its internal space very effectively with high-quality fixtures and fittings.

Finally, after many more meetings and deliberations, a complete design was realised. This design would undergo minor alterations as planning continued, but major design features, such as the mezzanine and glass extension would remain the same (Figs 7–9).

It was important throughout each stage of planning to address every aspect of the design and not leave any stone unturned – no matter how small – so every minute part of the build and internal design in the final realisation had been carefully thought through and discussed. These discussions were planned to strict deadlines, enabling each stage of the build to begin on time. Each part of the building process relied upon the completion of the previous part, so a delay at any point could have a costly knock-on effect.

So, we now had the blueprint of a new library...

Figs 7–9 – Artists impressions of the new library. © Pettorino Design

The development begins

The summer of 2015 saw the start of the library build. The floor of the gymnasium had been investigated earlier in the spring and it was discovered to be hollow underneath. This was excellent news as it meant the floor, currently accessed by two steps, could be lowered, not only giving additional height to the mezzanine but removing step access – essential for moving book trolleys from the store cupboard into the library.

And so the build began. I was privileged to have been given access to every stage of the build, and once a week I donned a high-viz jacket and hard hat and was taken by the site manager Peter Beilby on a tour of the latest stage in the library's development. I saw and photographed every stage of the build – an invaluable record for the school archives! (See Figs 10–13)

Fig. 10 (left) – Building the glass extension. Fig. 11 (right) – Floor lowered, new flooring in place, walls sandblasted and mezzanine structure erected. Photos by Lynn Winkworth.

I have many happy memories of regularly climbing the scaffolding ladder onto the shell of the mezzanine; of watching from inside as the glass extension took shape and of seeing all the amazing wiring and insulation installed; of very cold, dark frosty mornings in the winter months when the build was only lit by construction lamps, through to the spring of 2016 when heating and lighting were warming and illuminating the interior.

These weekly visits onsite were invaluable. They enabled me not only to understand how the new library was constructed from the ground up, but also to ask questions as the build progressed. Thanks must go to Peter Beilby, who managed the build, for the time he spent with me each week, and the patience he demonstrated in answering my questions every Friday morning. These weekly meetings continued until the new library was complete, and the keys handed over to the Bursar.

Whilst the physical space was being built, the basic internal design continued to be discussed and tweaked. This was not finalised until the physical fitments were commissioned in the spring of 2016. Serota – a firm specialising in building bespoke library furniture – were engaged to undertake this part of the build, creating study desks and oak bookshelves to our exact specification.

Fig. 12 (left) – Up on the mezzanine! Fig. 13 (right) – Internal structure taking shape. Photos by Lynn Winkworth.

Whilst all the above was happening, the old library had to be prepared for moving to its new location. From the beginning we knew the library would be moving to a smaller space and therefore a significant reduction in book stock would be required. We calculated the capacity of the new library once we had finalised the design – we would need to reduce our physical resources by around 49%. Planning a weed of such significant size is not a task to be underestimated and before we began there were many hours of careful planning and discussion. As you can imagine, a great deal of physical work would be needed before the library could be relocated to its new home.

So, how did we do it?

Decommissioning the old library

At Headington School sixth-form students have the opportunity to study either the IB or A levels and may additionally opt to undertake the Extended Project Qualification. It was essential the new library collections continued to fully support these, along with Key Stages 3 and 4 specifications currently taught within the curriculum. Staff research needs and wider reading requirements were also taken into consideration.

I spent many hours looking at weeding criteria before we began. Loan statistics and individual accession records were very useful – but only as a starting point. I looked in detail at the wide range of electronic resources we held, including the introduction of eBooks in support of our fiction collection, and looked where duplication lay. From running research sessions I had developed a detailed knowledge of which resources would need to remain in place, but this knowledge was not sufficient alone.

To complete the process successfully required an intimate knowledge of subject specifications held only by the teaching staff. It was therefore arranged that every department would come and ruthlessly weed their own collections, leaving only key resources behind. Before the weeded stock was permanently removed, I looked at each book to retain those which from experience I knew to be wider reading, cross-curricular or used in specific research projects (referring to reading lists I had previously created). Any of the withdrawn titles still deemed of interest by departments were taken to their department. I must thank the teaching staff at this stage, for without their detailed subject knowledge and support it would have been impossible to have weeded the collections as accurately as we did. (See Fig. 14)

Fig 14 - Piles of weeded books ready for processing. Photo by Lynn Winkworth.

It was essential that book stock figures were accurate throughout the weeding process. Weed too little and the collections would not physically fit into the new library space. Weed too far and we would not only have empty bookshelves in the new library, but the collections would become damaged and academic support would be compromised; this I was not prepared to do. I built a small amount of growth space into the final figures – essential for further collection development.

I kept a detailed spreadsheet of book stock figures during this time to aid this process. However, the final number was determined by yet another manual count of every remaining book to ensure, beyond doubt, the book stock would fit into its new home. My thanks at this stage must go to two of my close colleagues, who helped tirelessly with the weeding and counting of the book stock. It would have been more than difficult to do it without you!

Withdrawn books no longer required in school were offered to staff and students. We created a shelving area of these books and students and staff were often seen perusing them. Many of the books were recycled in this way and those that were left were collected and sold through Betterworld Books, raising money to support girls' and women's education in Africa.

As with many libraries we hold resources in formats other than books, collections which also needed to be scaled down. Newspaper cuttings were no longer necessary in the way they once were – with Current Awareness and Historical news events now freely available online most of the physical archive was removed.

Our extensive DVD Collection was also significantly weeded. Now that films can be readily streamed, films in DVD format are in less demand. We therefore trimmed the collection to meet curriculum specifications, with a small number of social films remaining to continue to support student enjoyment across all Key Stages. The collection of audiobooks and music CDs, now so rarely borrowed, were transferred to the English and Music Departments respectively.

Every item that was removed from the library was duly counted, removed from the catalogue and updated to show it was withdrawn stock. This in itself was a mammoth task, but essential if our library catalogue was to continue to accurately reflect the library collection.

Preparing for the library moving

Once the weeding was completed, we turned our attention to the remaining books. The original library had two separate classification sequences and to combine them would previously have been logistically unfeasible. Due to the space created from the weed this could now be done. To amalgamate the two classifications into one we needed to move the entire non-fiction collection. It took two of us many hours to complete, but was well worth the effort!

The fiction collection, shelved in a separate room, could now also be transferred into the main library area. This would leave this room empty, allowing it to be used for pupil study during the week of the library move.

It was important that the library was in the correct classification sequence prior to moving, so every shelf was then checked in detail for the correct order. Once this had been completed, but before the library could be moved, we needed to map the old library to the new. The classification must flow seamlessly, so it was crucial to carefully visualise the stock layout in the new location.

RFID and technology

We decided to upgrade the library security system from electromagnetic to Radio Frequency Identification (RFID), allowing us to install a self-issue and return kiosk system often found in university libraries. This system would email users details of every book they issued or returned.

In order for the new RFID system to be put in place, all library resources had to be fitted with a smart programmable security tag. It was essential this was completed before the library move, so a tagging team were engaged to undertake this three-day task. We ensured that books on loan were tagged upon return.

The new library would also include an 84-inch interactive table, suitable for ten students to use simultaneously in support of collaborative learning. The teaching area would house a monitor of the same size that could be used to employ the latest technology for teaching and learning. The mezzanine would be a dedicated computer area, where a mixture of Macs and PCs would be installed.

A computer help station was to be sited at the back of the library where students could book an individual IT session with our dedicated IT team. Programmable digital signage at the entrance to the library and above the help station would inform users of school- and library-specific events.

It was decided the library would become a pilot for Beacon Technology, where information could be pushed to iPads and smartphones on entering the library. This information would not only support students' learning, but would serve to highlight new resources and other library news.

Two high-tech sonic chairs – pod-like spheres that allow music and spoken word to be listened to free from headphones but without disturbing others – would be installed in the glass extension.

Moving the library

I discovered there are only a few companies who specialise in moving libraries and after much research Harrow Green, the London based specialist removal firm, were employed to undertake this task. I was impressed with their professional approach to moving the library, especially of the consideration they demonstrated to working within the school environment. (See Fig. 15, right)

Over the course of four days early in May 2016 the team of around ten people successfully moved the library to its new home.

Promoting the new library

While the new library was being built the architect's designs were displayed for the school community and prospective parents to see. A promotional video, using a 'fly-through' technique (see Figs 7–9 above, and video link at the end of this article), allowed prospective users to see a three-dimensional rendering of the new library. Engaging the school community in this way meant students and staff had a genuine interest and excitement in seeing the new library come to life.

The library finally opened to users on Wednesday 10th May 2016 (see Figs 16a and b). It was met with great excitement, and is proving to be just as popular, if not more so, than before.

Figs 16a and b – Library opening day. Photos by Lynn Winkworth.

The library today

The library at Headington School is first and foremost a learning environment, with the expectation that no one hinders the learning of others. It is made up of four distinct areas, each with its own specialism – and these areas would develop a character of their own the more they were used.

Fig. 17 (above) – The large extension. Fig. 18 (right) – The main area of the library. Photos by Lynn Winkworth.

The large glass extension, where the fiction collection is shelved, is our reading for pleasure area. Here you will find ten large, comfy chairs, glass coffee tables and a sofa brought from the old library. Two study desks and the sonic chairs complete the furnishings – the sonic chairs are a particular favourite! The texture and colour of the unique flooring matches the grass of the quad, merging the inside with the out. The atmosphere here is one of relaxation, quiet conversation and, at times, peacefulness. On all sides solar blinds can be deployed to shade from morning and evening sun – essential for comfortable working! (See Fig. 17).

Fig. 19 (above) – The mezzanine floor in use.
Fig. 20 (below) – Teaching in the silent study room. Photos by Lynn Winkworth.

The main area of the library – complete with large tables for collaborative working, interactive table and IT support area – is the central hub from which all other areas are accessed. Here you find the library desk and part of our non-fiction collections. It is a busy, vibrant area of the library, quite different from other parts. Solar blinds are also installed above the large windows on the west side of this room. (see Fig. 18)

The mezzanine floor is reached by ascending the sweeping staircase, with its bespoke glass balustrade, and is surrounded by medium-height glass walls. There are 38 seats and the 18 computers are always in high demand. Solar blinds on the high-level windows allow us to shade the screens from glare. The atmosphere of the upper deck, as we call it, and its brand new computers is one of inspiration for research and contemporary learning. The height of the deck gives it a unique feeling of being separate but still part of the library environment. (see Fig. 19)

The silent study room is separated from the main area by a wall of glass and is accessed by two huge glass doors. The atmosphere as you enter immediately changes into one of concentration and focused academic study. Here we also shelve non-fiction collections. Along with private study, this area is used for teaching, after-school film screenings, school council meetings, scholarship events and so on. (see Fig. 20)

Some finishing touches needed to happen after the library had opened, as some details could only be finalised once the library was operating on a day-to-day basis. Glass coffee tables were installed in the extension to complement the fiction area; in the main study room purposefully designed tables and new green chairs replaced the temporary ones; a charging station has been installed; and another single collaborative table, replacing two smaller ones, completed the main area of the library.

The new self-issue and return system has proved very successful. When a user issues a book at the self-issue kiosk or returns a book at the return kiosk, their records are automatically updated and an email confirmation is sent. For this system to work effectively, not only must every resource include a smart tag, but it is essential every user has a library card. For the first week we opened we therefore provided free replacement library cards to those users who had lost theirs – needless to say, this proved a great success!

We can now use RFID for stocktaking, locating misshelved items and improved stock management. The users enjoy the independence of issue and return and are benefitting from learning new skills.

The library, now sited at the heart of the building, is one of the busiest areas in school, being used from 7:30 in the morning to 6:00 at night. It is now open three days a week outside these hours in support of the boarding community. The initial excitement of the library opening has given way to focused learning, with often over 100 students using it during the day. The library not only supports and encourages academic achievements, but is an area the whole school community can use and enjoy.

Conclusion

When we were designing and developing the new library we knew it was essential for the space to work not only as a fully-functioning library, offering comfortable academic workspaces, but also as an area for relaxation and reading for pleasure. It is clear from the response of students and staff alike that this goal has been achieved.

The design of the new library is sympathetic to its new location, and many original features have been retained and enhanced. The original painted walls were sandblasted to reveal a wonderful warm red brickwork, original lintels were left unpainted and metal roof trusses – previously unobtrusive – now proudly stand out against the newly insulated vaulted ceiling.

We took an underused space and transformed it into a state-of-the-art school library – a library that will support and encourage academic learning for many years to come. It truly does have the 'wow factor' we were aiming for!

Early in 2017 I applied to the School Library Association for the new library to be considered for the prestigious SLA Inspiration Award.

The judges said:

> 'Careful thought has been given to different ways of learning and smart technology has been wrapped into the design ranging from a touch screen table to sonic chairs, giving an offer that is balanced, non-intrusive and flexible. This vision includes how it can free the Librarian's time from clerical tasks to performing the valued work of teaching and supporting pupils and staff. The ethos is excellent with a high standard of practice and provision which together form an excellent school library model for the 21st Century.'

On 2 October 2017 the library at Headington School was awarded, along with two other schools, the **School Library Association Inspiration Award for 2017** for an outstanding contribution to innovation, creativity and resourcefulness in School Library design and use.

This adventure is complete, but the library is a living, breathing entity that should never remain still... so the next adventure is about to begin!

And finally...

The Planning - The Practicalities - The Opening: Three 'Check-lists' to help you along the way

Section 1: The Planning

➤ Be certain of your vision for your new library

➤ Use your professional knowledge to enhance the creation of your new library

➤ Be open to suggestions and make suggestions

➤ Think widely and 'outside the box' – is there something innovative you can do?

➤ Ask many questions – leave no stone unturned. Think yourself around the new library space and miss nothing

➤ Research, research and research again – you are only likely to move a library once and you really want to get it right first time

➤ Ask yourself - are there any issues in the current design that need addressing in the new one – now is the time to do it and to get it right

➤ Consider site lines in the new library – what can you see, are book cases blocking your vision of certain spaces, how well will students be able to move around your new design?

➤ Consider carefully where you are going to place your library desk – what parts of the library can you see from the position you have chosen?

➤ Keep records, detailing every part of the process from start to finish

➤ Create overarching development plans – review, update and recreate. Do not discard the original ones – they could still hold useful information

➤ Carefully think through the times scale from start to completion

➤ Carefully think through the order you need to do things in – it is important to get it right as everything will feed into everything else.

➤ Be aware of planning deadlines – penalties can be called upon if decision deadlines are missed

➤ Be involved in the build itself by having regular meetings with the site manager – seeing the library develop from the ground up is an amazing experience and gives you the opportunity to ask questions and to ask again and some more!

➤ Think about how you will manage not only your library space but also the students under your care.

Section 2: The Practicalities

➤ Have you analysed in detail the space available in the new library area – are you happy with it?

➤ Have you mapped your books to the new space? Be aware that you do not map the books 'backwards' – think yourself physically shelving and moving around the library

➤ Are your books currently in the same order as they will be in the new library – if not, consider moving resources in the existing library to reflect the order you require in the new one.